Great Job!

Achie Award

T0273148

_____

(name)

has completed

Let's Leap Ahead

Kindergarten

Learning while having fun!

on

_____

(date)

Hurray!   **Well done!**

Congratulations!

Alphabet

Fun with A! Practice writing the uppercase letter "A."
Complete the words below and find the missing sticker.

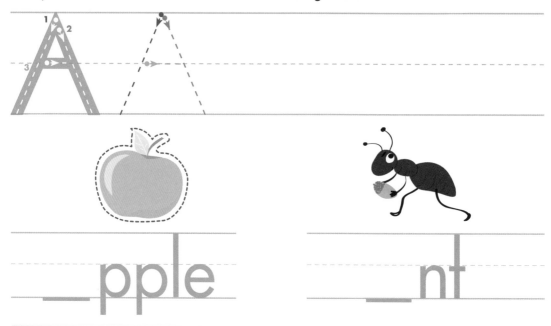

___pple   ___nt

Fun with a! Practice writing the lowercase letter "a."
Complete the words below and find the missing sticker.

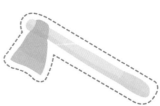

___irplane   ___xe

Alphabet

Fun with B! Practice writing the uppercase letter "B."
Complete the words below and find the missing sticker.

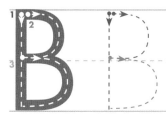

__room

__all

Fun with b! Practice writing the lowercase letter "b."
Complete the words below and find the missing sticker.

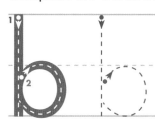

__ell

__ear

Alphabet

Fun with C! Practice writing the uppercase letter "C."
Complete the words below and find the missing sticker.

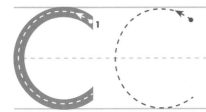

___ow

___ake

Fun with c! Practice writing the lowercase letter "c."
Complete the words below and find the missing sticker.

___up

___orn

Alphabet

Fun with D! Practice writing the uppercase letter "D."
Complete the words below and find the missing sticker.

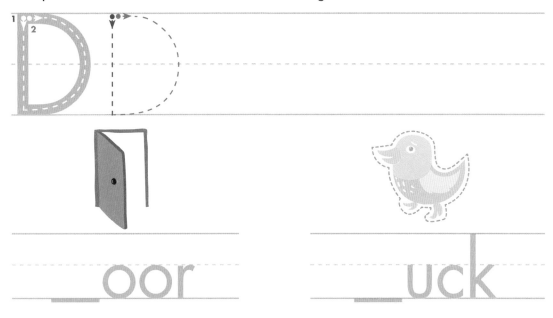

___oor   ___uck

Fun with d! Practice writing the lowercase letter "d."
Complete the words below and find the missing sticker.

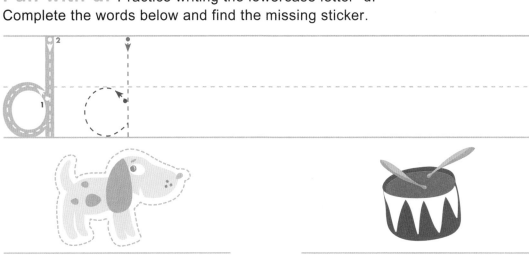

___og   ___rum

Alphabet

Fun with E! Practice writing the uppercase letter "E."
Complete the words below and find the missing sticker.

_agle   __ye

Fun with e! Practice writing the lowercase letter "e."
Complete the words below and find the missing sticker.

_arth   _lephant

Alphabet

Fun with F! Practice writing the uppercase letter "F."
Complete the words below and find the missing sticker.

＿ork   ＿ish

Fun with f! Practice writing the lowercase letter "f."
Complete the words below and find the missing sticker.

＿an   ＿rog

Alphabet

Fun with G! Practice writing the uppercase letter "G."
Complete the words below and find the missing sticker.

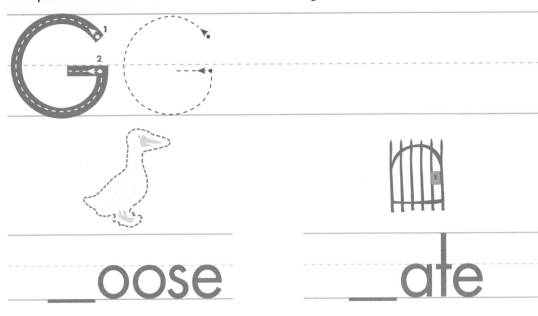

___oose

___ate

Fun with g! Practice writing the lowercase letter "g."
Complete the words below and find the missing sticker.

___ift

___oat

Alphabet

Fun with H! Practice writing the uppercase letter "H."
Complete the words below and find the missing sticker.

___ouse

___orn

Fun with h! Practice writing the lowercase letter "h."
Complete the words below and find the missing sticker.

___en

___at

Fun with I! Practice writing the uppercase letter "I."
Complete the words below and find the missing sticker.

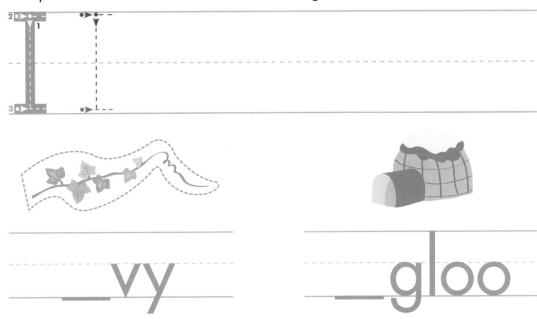

__vy   __gloo

Fun with i! Practice writing the lowercase letter "i."
Complete the words below and find the missing sticker.

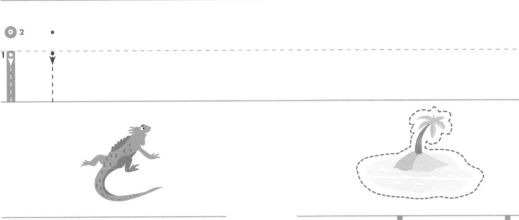

__guana   __sland

Alphabet

Fun with J! Practice writing the uppercase letter "J."
Complete the words below and find the missing sticker.

J J

_ellyfish   _eans

Fun with j! Practice writing the lowercase letter "j."
Complete the words below and find the missing sticker.

j j

_ug   _am

Alphabet

Fun with K! Practice writing the uppercase letter "K."
Complete the words below and find the missing sticker.

___ing   ___ey

Fun with k! Practice writing the lowercase letter "k."
Complete the words below and find the missing sticker.

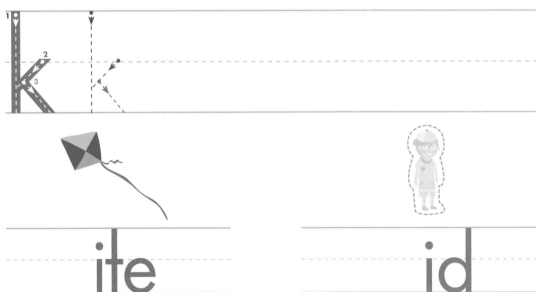

___ite   ___id

Alphabet

Fun with L! Practice writing the uppercase letter "L."
Complete the words below and find the missing sticker.

___eaf

___obster

Fun with l! Practice writing the lowercase letter "l."
Complete the words below and find the missing sticker.

___ion

___og

Fun with M! Practice writing the uppercase letter "M."
Complete the words below and find the missing sticker.

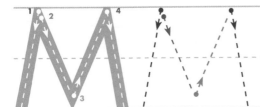

 __uffin

 __ouse

Fun with m! Practice writing the lowercase letter "m."
Complete the words below and find the missing sticker.

 __op

 __oon

Alphabet

Fun with N! Practice writing the uppercase letter "N."
Complete the words below and find the missing sticker.

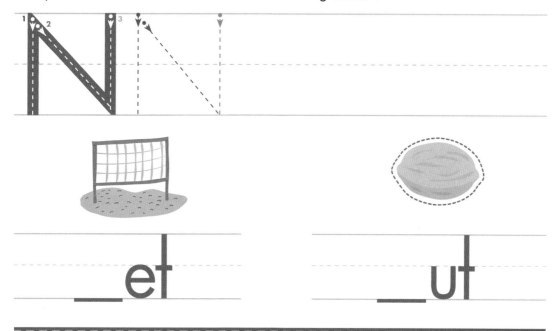

__et   __ut

Fun with n! Practice writing the lowercase letter "n."
Complete the words below and find the missing sticker.

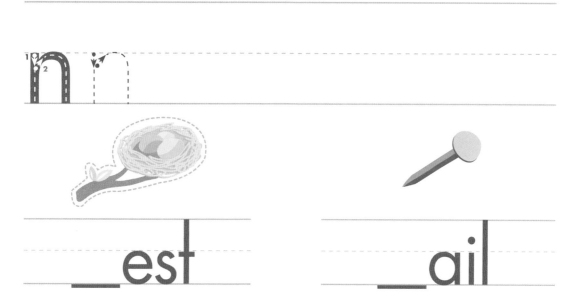

__est   __ail

Alphabet

Fun with O! Practice writing the uppercase letter "O."
Complete the words below and find the missing sticker.

___wl   ___nion

Fun with o! Practice writing the lowercase letter "o."
Complete the words below and find the missing sticker.

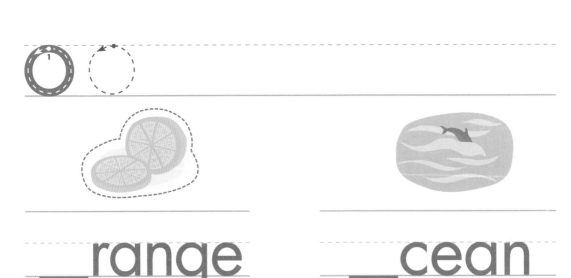

___range   ___cean

Alphabet

Fun with P! Practice writing the uppercase letter "P."
Complete the words below and find the missing sticker.

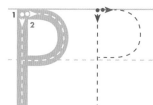

__enguin   __eas

Fun with p! Practice writing the lowercase letter "p."
Complete the words below and find the missing sticker.

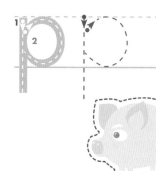

__ig   __encil

Fun with Q! Practice writing the uppercase letter "Q."
Complete the words below and find the missing sticker.

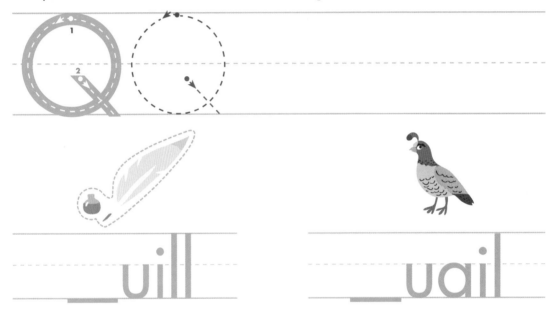

__uill

__uail

Fun with q! Practice writing the lowercase letter "q."
Complete the words below and find the missing sticker.

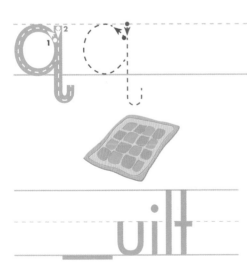

__uilt

__ueen

Fun with R! Practice writing the uppercase letter "R."
Complete the words below and find the missing sticker.

 _abbit

_ing

Fun with r! Practice writing the lowercase letter "r."
Complete the words below and find the missing sticker.

_ose

_uler

Fun with S! Practice writing the uppercase letter "S."
Complete the words below and find the missing sticker.

_un   _carf

Fun with s! Practice writing the lowercase letter "s."
Complete the words below and find the missing sticker.

_tar   _aw

Alphabet

Fun with T! Practice writing the uppercase letter "T."
Complete the words below and find the missing sticker.

__ree   __ie

Fun with t! Practice writing the lowercase letter "t."
Complete the words below and find the missing sticker.

__urtle   __rain

Fun with U! Practice writing the uppercase letter "U."
Complete the words below and find the missing sticker.

U U

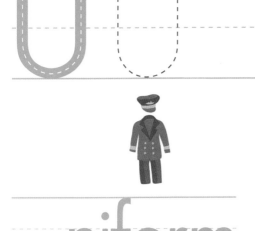

_niform

_nicorn

Fun with u! Practice writing the lowercase letter "u."
Complete the words below and find the missing sticker.

u u

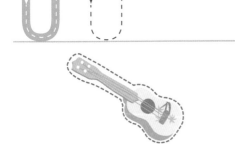

_kulele

_nicycle

Fun with V! Practice writing the uppercase letter "V."
Complete the words below and find the missing sticker.

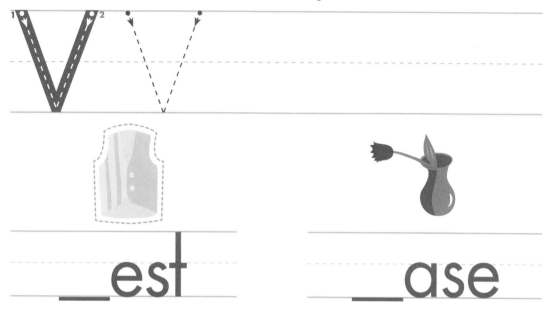

__est   __ase

Fun with v! Practice writing the lowercase letter "v."
Complete the words below and find the missing sticker.

__olcano   __iolin

Alphabet

Fun with W! Practice writing the uppercase letter "W."
Complete the words below and find the missing sticker.

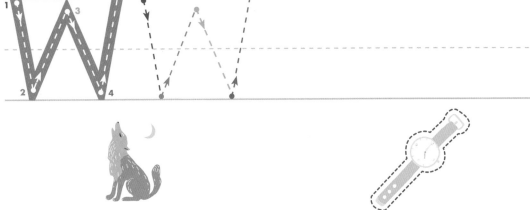

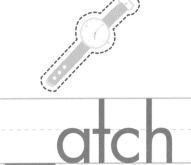

_olf   _atch

Fun with w! Practice writing the lowercase letter "w."
Complete the words below and find the missing sticker.

_histle   _hale

Alphabet

Fun with X! Practice writing the uppercase letter "X."
Complete the words below and find the missing sticker.

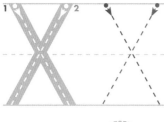

_enops   _-ray

Fun with x! Practice writing the lowercase letter "x."
Complete the words below and find the missing sticker.

bo_   fo_

Alphabet

Fun with Y! Practice writing the uppercase letter "Y."
Complete the words below and find the missing sticker.

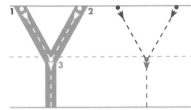

___am

_ellow

Fun with y! Practice writing the lowercase letter "y."
Complete the words below and find the missing sticker.

_ard

_arn

Fun with Z! Practice writing the uppercase letter "Z."
Complete the words below and find the missing sticker.

_ucchini   _ebra

Fun with z! Practice writing the lowercase letter "z."
Complete the words below and find the missing sticker.

_ipper   _oo

Alphabet

At the beach! Write the missing letters.

Alphabet

On the farm! Write the missing letters.

⬜utterflies

⬜est

⬜uck

fo⬜

⬜ig

⬜uail

Numbers

Fun with 1! Trace the "1" and practice writing it.
Then trace the word and find the missing sticker.

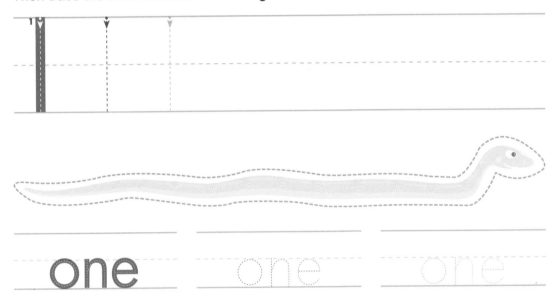

Fun with 2! Trace the "2" and practice writing it.
Then trace the word and find the missing sticker.

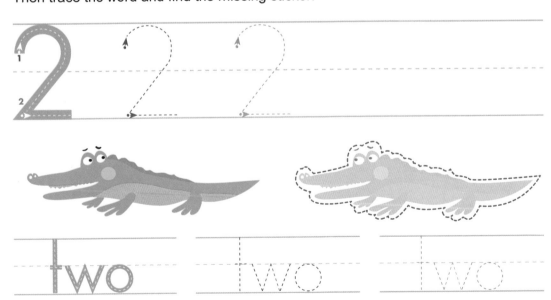

Numbers

Fun with 3! Trace the "3" and practice writing it.
Then trace the word and find the missing sticker.

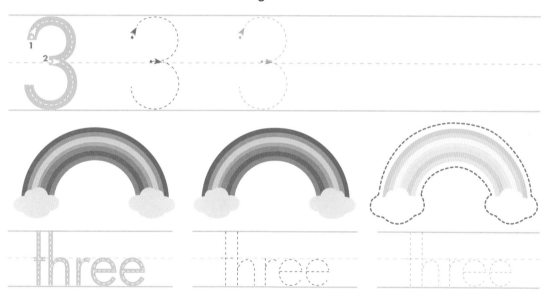

Fun with 4! Trace the "4" and practice writing it.
Then trace the word and find the missing sticker.

Fun with 5! Trace the "5" and practice writing it.
Then trace the word and find the missing sticker.

five   five   five

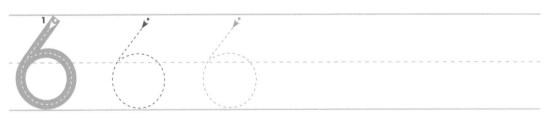

Fun with 6! Trace the "6" and practice writing it.
Then trace the word and find the missing sticker.

six six   six

Numbers

Fun with 7! Trace the "7" and practice writing it. Then trace the word and find the missing sticker.

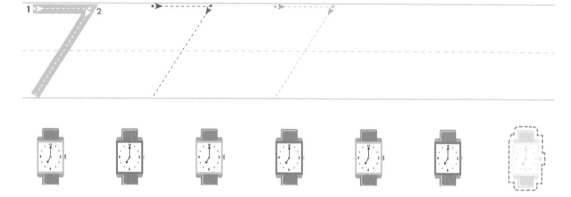

seven seven seven

Fun with 8! Trace the "8" and practice writing it. Then trace the word and find the missing sticker.

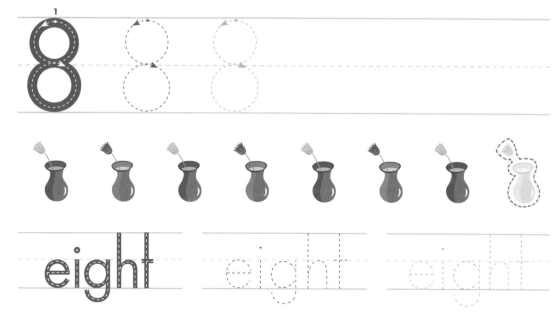

eight eight eight

Numbers

Fun with 9! Trace the "9" and practice writing it. Then trace the word and find the missing sticker.

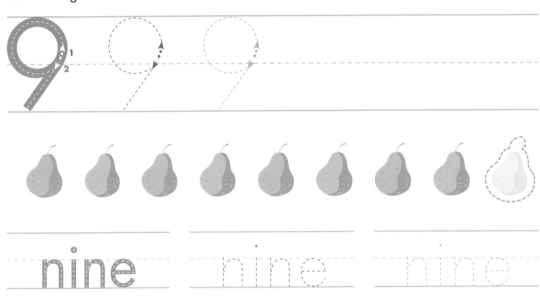

Fun with 10! Trace the "10" and practice writing it. Then trace the word and find the missing sticker.

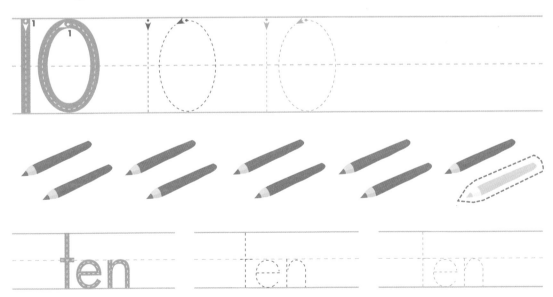

Colors

Learning Colors! Trace the words "red," "yellow," and "blue."

red   yellow   blue

Learning Colors! Trace the words "orange," "purple," and "green."

orange purple green

Colors

Learning Colors! Trace the words "teal," "pink," and "black."

Learning Colors! Trace the words "brown," "lime," and "white."

Colors

Finding Colors! Circle the red cherries and the yellow bananas.

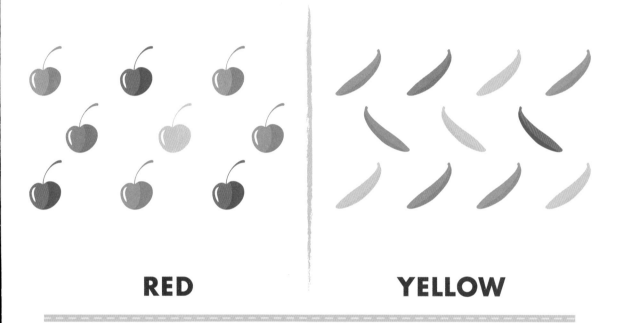

RED   **YELLOW**

Finding Colors! Circle the green apples and the blue blueberries.

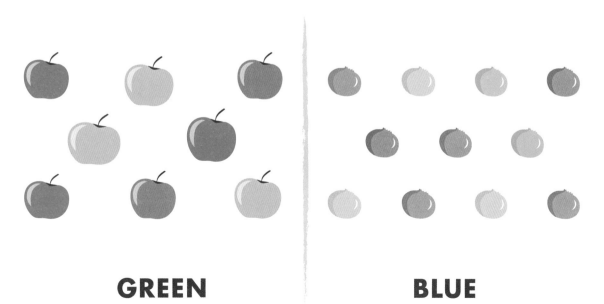

GREEN   **BLUE**

Finding Colors! Circle the orange oranges and the lime limes.

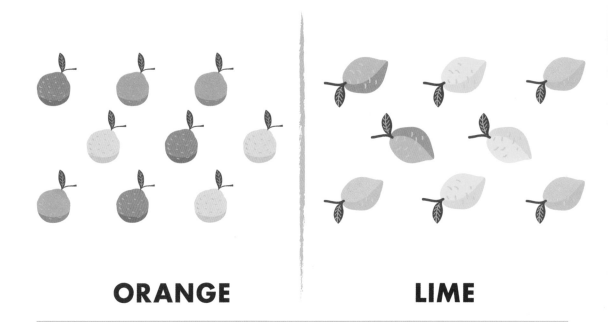

ORANGE   **LIME**

Finding Colors! Circle the purple eggplants and the teal forks.

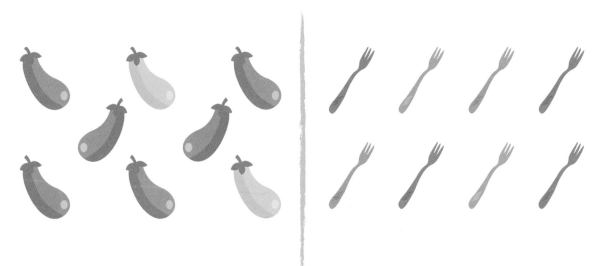

PURPLE   **TEAL**

Finding Colors! Circle the pink flowers and the black spiders.

PINK   BLACK

Finding Colors! Circle the white socks and the brown nuts.

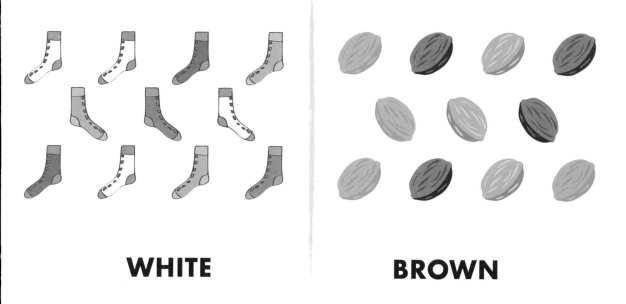

WHITE   BROWN

Colors

Matching Colors! Draw a line to match the objects that are the same color.

Matching Colors! Draw a line to match the objects that are the same color.

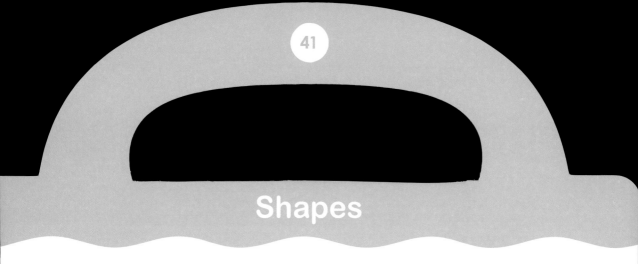

Shapes

Circle & Square! Trace the circle and the square. Then, trace the names of the shapes.

circle   square

Triangle & Rectangle! Trace the triangle and the rectangle. Then, trace the names of the shapes.

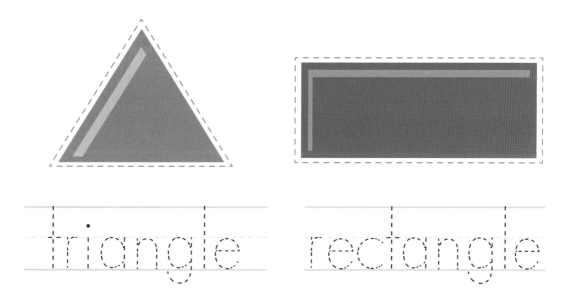

triangle   rectangle

Shapes

Diamond & Oval! Trace the diamond and the oval. Then, trace the names of the shapes.

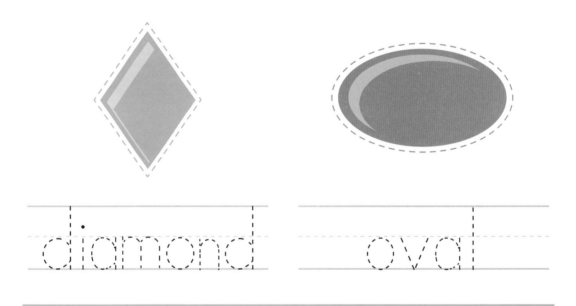

diamond   oval

Trapezoid & Star! Trace the trapezoid and the star. Then, trace the names of the shapes.

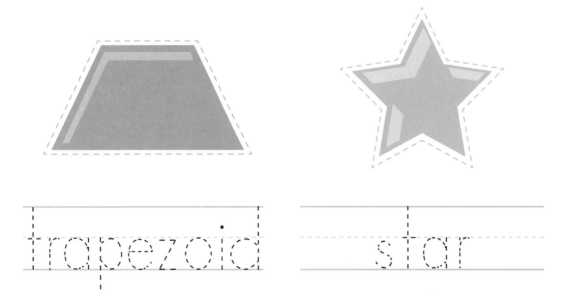

trapezoid   star

Shapes

Circle & Square! Circle the circles and the squares in the correct columns.

CIRCLE   **SQUARE**

Triangle & Rectangle! Circle the triangles and the rectangles in the correct columns.

TRIANGLE   **RECTANGLE**

Shapes

Diamond & Oval! Circle the diamonds and the ovals in the correct columns.

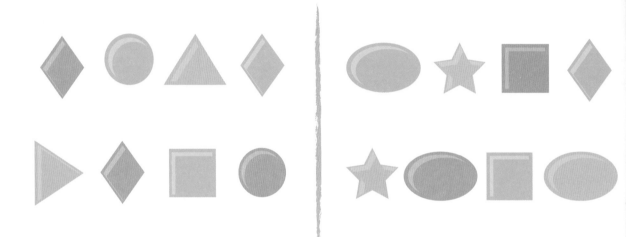

DIAMOND

OVAL

Trapezoid & Star! Circle the trapezoids and the stars in the correct columns.

TRAPEZOID

STAR

Sorting

Fun with Food! Find the missing sticker, then draw a line to match the foods that go together.

Fun with Sports! Find the missing sticker, then draw a line to match the sports things that go together.

Sorting

Fun with Seasons! Find the missing sticker, then draw a line to match the weather things that go together.

Fun with Animals! Find the missing sticker, then draw a line to match the animals and things that go together.

Sorting

Fun with School! Find the missing sticker, then draw a line to match the school things that go together.

Fun with Jobs! Find the missing sticker, then draw a line to match the jobs and things that go together.

Sorting

In Your Room! Circle the things that belong in your bedroom.
Cross out the things that don't belong in your bedroom.

In the Kitchen! Circle the things that belong in the kitchen.
Cross out the things that don't belong in the kitchen.

What Goes Next?

Learning Patterns!
Draw the things in the sky that should come next.

Learning Patterns!
Draw the things in the garden that should come next.

What Goes Next?

Learning Patterns!
Write the letters or numbers that should come next.

Learning Patterns!
Write the letters or numbers that should come next.

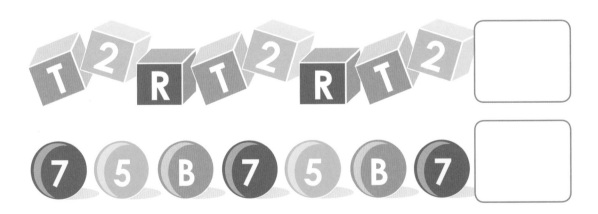

Comparisons

Most & Fewest! Circle the tree that has the most apples.
Underline the tree that has the fewest apples.

Tallest & Shortest! Circle the tallest building. Underline the shortest building.

Comparisons

Hottest & Coldest! Circle the hottest food. Underline the coldest food.

Biggest & Smallest! Circle the biggest animal. Underline the smallest animal.

Learning Vowels! These letters are vowels! Practice saying each letter aloud.

AEIOU and sometimes Y

and sometimes Y

Maze Craze! The vowels are having fun at the beach.
Follow the vowels through the maze to get to the sand.

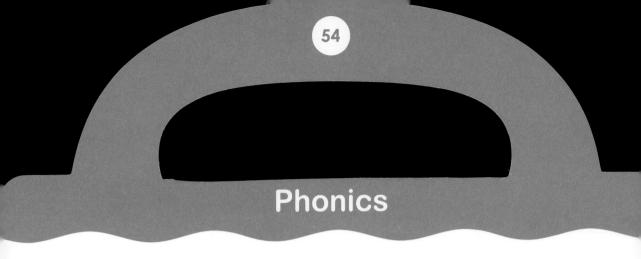

Phonics

Fun with Short A/a! Sometimes the letter "A/a" makes a "short" sound, like in "cat." Find the missing sticker, then circle all the things whose name makes a "short A/a" sound.

Fun with Long A/a! The letter "A/a" can make a "long" sound, like in "cake." Find the missing sticker, then circle all the things whose name makes a "long A/a" sound.

Phonics

Fun with Short E/e! Sometimes the letter "E/e" makes a "short" sound, like in "net." Find the missing sticker, then circle all the things whose name makes a "short E/e" sound.

Fun with Long E/e! Sometimes the letter "E/e" makes a "long" sound, like in "tree." Find the missing sticker, then circle all the things whose name makes a "long E/e" sound.

Phonics

Fun with Short I/i! Sometimes the letter "I/i" makes a "short" sound, like in "fish." Find the missing sticker, then circle all the things whose name makes a "short I/i" sound.

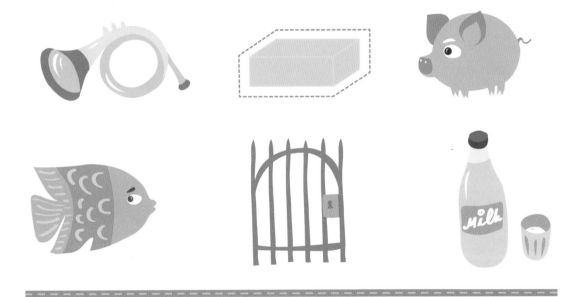

Fun with Long I/i! Sometimes the letter "I/i" makes a "long" sound, like in "slide." Find the missing sticker, then circle all the things whose name makes a "long I/i" sound.

Phonics

Fun with Short O/o! Sometimes the letter "O/o" makes a "short" sound, like in "sock." Find the missing sticker, then circle all the things whose name makes a "short O/o" sound.

Fun with Long O/o! Sometimes the letter "O/o" makes a "long" sound, like in "bone." Find the missing sticker, then circle all the things whose name makes a "long O/o" sound.

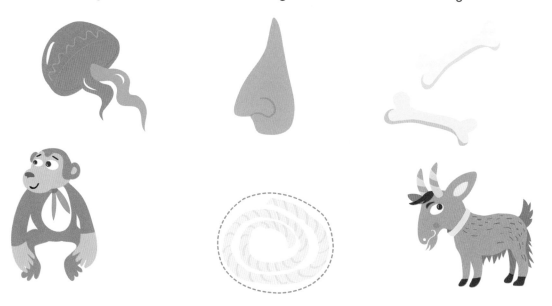

Phonics

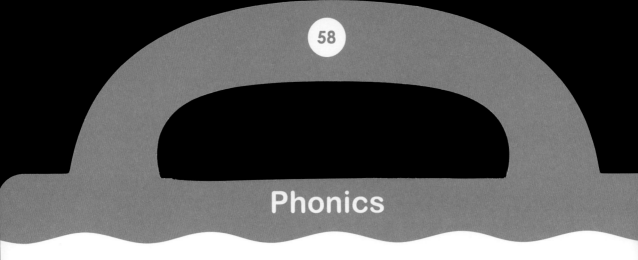

Fun with Short U/u! Sometimes the letter "U/u" makes a "short" sound, like in "bus." Find the missing sticker, then circle all the things whose name makes a "short U/u" sound.

Fun with Long U/u! Sometimes the letter "U/u" makes a "long" sound, like in "juice." Find the missing sticker, then circle all the things whose name makes a "long U/u" sound.

Phonics

Learning Consonants!
These letters are consonants! Say each letter aloud.

B C D F G H
J K L M N P Q
R S T V W X Y Z

Finding the B/b Sound!
Find the missing sticker, then circle all the things whose name makes a "B/b" sound, like "book."

Phonics

Finding the Hard C/c Sound! Sometimes the letter "C/c" makes a "hard" sound, like in "car." Find the missing sticker, then circle all the things whose name makes a "hard C/c" sound.

Finding the Soft C/c Sound! Sometimes the letter "C/c" makes a "soft" sound, like in "city." Find the missing sticker, then circle all the things whose name makes a "soft C/c" sound.

Phonics

Finding the D/d Sound! Find the missing sticker, then circle all the things whose name makes a "D/d" sound, like "dolphin."

Finding the F/f Sound! Find the missing sticker, then circle all the things whose name makes an "F/f" sound, like "fan."

Phonics

Finding the Hard G/g Sound! Sometimes the letter "G/g" makes a "hard" sound, like in "grapes." Find the missing sticker, tthen circle all the things whose name makes a "hard G/g" sound.

Finding the Soft G/g Sound! Sometimes the letter "G/g" makes a "soft" sound, like in "gem." Find the missing sticker, then circle all the things whose name makes a "soft G/g" sound.

Phonics

Finding the H/h Sound! Find the missing sticker, then circle all the things whose name makes an "H/h" sound, like "hippo."

Finding the J/j Sound! Find the missing sticker, then circle all the things whose name makes a "J/j" sound, like "jar."

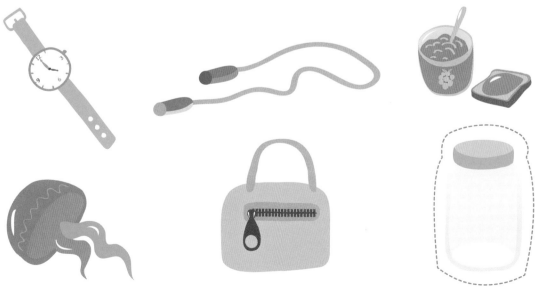

Phonics

Finding the K/k Sound! Find the missing sticker, then circle all the things whose name makes a "K/k" sound, like "king."

Finding the L/l Sound! Find the missing sticker, then circle all the things whose name makes an "L/l" sound, like "lettuce."

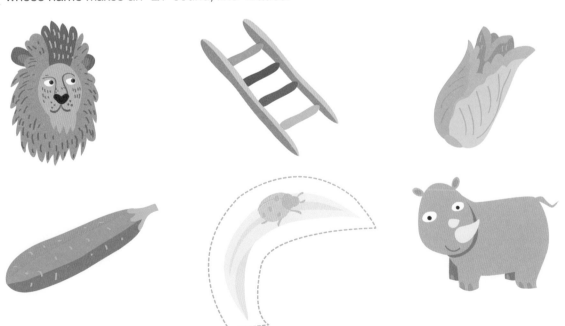

Phonics

Finding the M/m Sound! Find the missing sticker, then circle all the things whose name makes an "M/m" sound, like "map."

Finding the N/n Sound! Find the missing sticker, then circle all the things whose name makes an "N/n" sound, like "nest."

Phonics

Finding the P/p Sound! Find the missing sticker, then circle all the things whose name makes a "P/p" sound, like "pig."

Finding the Q/q Sound! Find the missing sticker, then circle all the things whose name makes a "Q/q" sound, like "quail."

Phonics

Finding the R/r Sound! Find the missing sticker, then circle all the things whose name makes an "R/r" sound, like "rocket."

Finding the S/s Sound! Find the missing sticker, then circle all the things whose name makes an "S/s" sound, like "scissors."

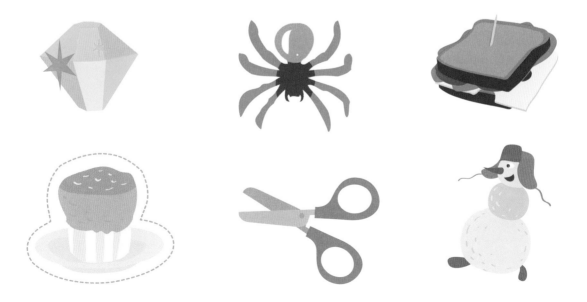

Phonics

Finding the T/t Sound! Find the missing sticker, then circle all the things whose name makes a "T/t" sound, like "tomato."

Finding the V/v Sound! Find the missing sticker, then circle all the things whose name makes a "V/v" sound, like "vase."

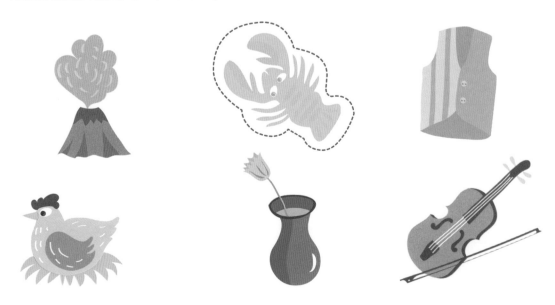

Phonics

Finding the W/w Sound! Find the missing sticker, then circle all the things whose name makes a "W/w" sound, like "watermelon."

Finding the X/x Sound! Find the missing sticker, then circle all the things whose name makes an "X/x" sound, like "fox."

Phonics

Finding the Y/y Sound! Find the missing sticker, then circle all the things whose name makes a "Y/y" sound, like "yarn."

Finding the Z/z Sound! Find the missing sticker, then circle all the things whose name makes a "Z/z" sound, like "zebra."

Counting

Counting Fruit! Count the fruit in each tree. Then, write the numbers below.

Counting Fruit! Uh-oh! A piece of fruit has fallen off of each tree. Count the fruit in each tree now.

Counting

Counting Bones! Count the bones around each doghouse. Then, write the numbers below.

Counting Bones! Dan the Dog has added a bone to each doghouse. Count the bones around each doghouse now.

Sight Words

Learning "an"
Trace the word "an." Then, write the word to complete the sentences.

 I have ___ apple.   He sees ___ owl.

 She is ___ artist.   We want ___ egg.

Learning "at"
Trace the word "at." Then, write the word to complete the sentences.

I am ___ school.   She is ___ the library.

He is ___ home.   They're ___ the park.

Sight Words

Learning "to"
Trace the word "to." Then, write the word to complete the sentences.

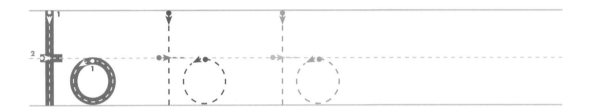

We go ___ the store.   I walk ___ the farm.

He likes ___ sing.   She likes ___ play.

Learning "of"
Trace the word "of." Then, write the word to complete the sentences.

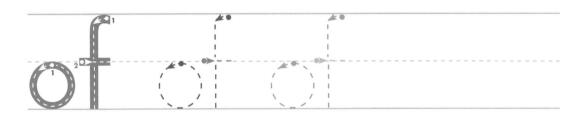

I have six ___ them.   We get out ___ the car.

The sky is full ___ stars.   We eat a lot ___ carrots.

Rhyming

Rhyme Time! Words that sound alike are rhyming words.
Circle the words that rhyme with "cat."

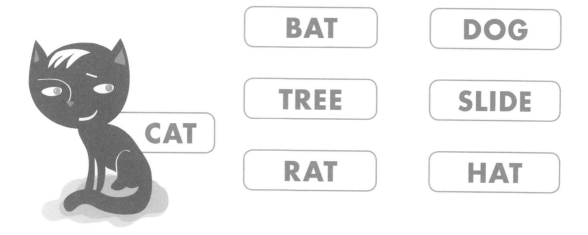

CAT

BAT DOG

TREE SLIDE

RAT HAT

Rhyme Time! Words that sound alike are rhyming words.
Circle the words that rhyme with "king."

KING

SUN SWING

RING JUICE

BIKE STRING

Rhyming

Rhyme Time! Words that sound alike are rhyming words.
Circle the words that rhyme with "clock."

CLOCK

CANE   ROCK

BLOCK   LAMP

QUEEN   SOCK

Rhyme Time! Words that sound alike are rhyming words.
Circle the words that rhyme with "bride."

BRIDE

SLIDE   HIDE

BANANA   PEN

GOOSE   RIDE

Telling Time

Learning Time! Trace the big hand and the little hand in the clocks below. Then, trace the time that each clock says.

Learning Time! Trace the big hand and the little hand in the clocks below. Then, trace the time that each clock says.

Telling Time

Matching Time! Do you know what time it is?
Draw a line to match each clock with the correct time.

11:00   12:00   10:00   9:00

Matching Time! Do you know what time it is?
Draw a line to match each clock with the correct time.

4:00   7:00   6:00   1:00

Telling Time

Telling Time! Do you know what time it is?
Draw the big hand and the little hand on each clock to show the correct time.

1:00   8:00   2:00   10:00

Telling Time! Do you know what time it is?
Draw the big hand and the little hand on each clock to show the correct time.

3:00   6:00   9:00   12:00

Telling Time

Telling Time! Do you know what time it is?
Write the correct time below each clock.

: _____   : _____   : _____   : _____

Telling Time! Do you know what time it is?
Write the correct time below each clock.

: _____   : _____   : _____   : _____

Money

Learning Coins! A penny is worth 1 cent.
Count the coins in each jar. Then, write the number of cents on the lines below.

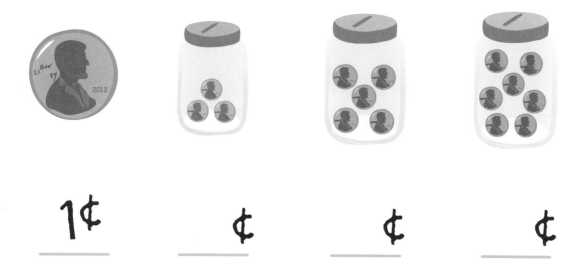

1¢   ____ ¢   ____ ¢   ____ ¢

Learning Coins! A nickel is worth 5 pennies, or 5 cents.
Count the coins in each jar. Then, write the number of cents on the lines below.

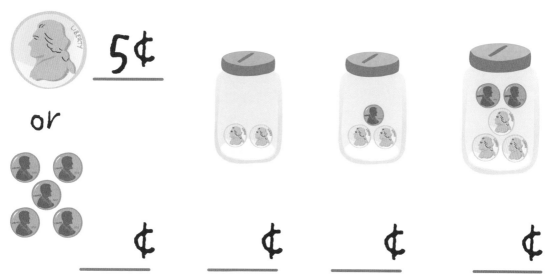

5¢

or

____ ¢   ____ ¢   ____ ¢   ____ ¢

Money

Learning Coins! A dime is worth 2 nickels, or 10 cents.
Count the coins in each jar. Then, write the number of cents on the lines below.

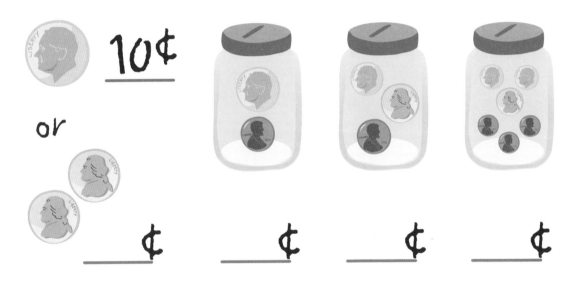

10¢

or

_____ ¢   _____ ¢   _____ ¢   _____ ¢

Learning Coins! A quarter is worth 2 dimes and 1 nickel, or 25 cents.
Count the coins in each jar. Then, write the number of cents on the lines below.

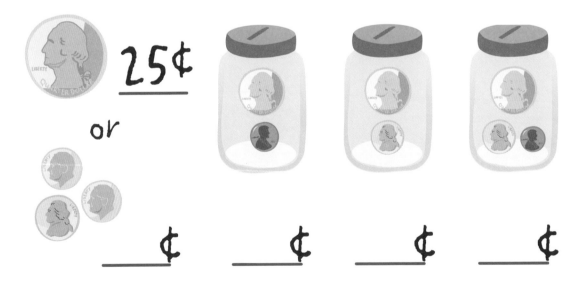

25¢

or

_____ ¢   _____ ¢   _____ ¢   _____ ¢

Science

Fun with the 5 Senses! Find the missing sticker, then circle the things that feel soft.

Fun with the 5 Senses! Find the missing sticker, then circle the things that have a strong smell.

Science

Fun with the 5 Senses! Find the missing sticker, then circle the things you can see, but not touch.

Fun with the 5 Senses! Find the missing sticker, then circle the things that make sounds.

Science

Fun with the 5 Senses! Find the missing sticker, then circle the things that taste good.

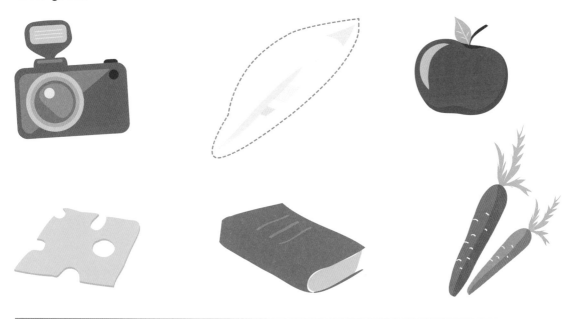

Fun with the 5 Senses! Check off the senses you use for each object.

	👂	👁	👃	👄	✋
🍕					
✈					
🎸					

Science

Finding Mammals! Animals with hair or fur are mammals. Even you are a mammal! Find the missing sticker, then circle all the mammals you see.

Finding Birds! Animals with feathers are birds. Find the missing sticker, then circle all the birds you see.

Science

Finding Reptiles! Animals that are cold blooded and have scales are reptiles. Find the missing sticker, then circle all the reptiles you see.

Finding Fish! Animals that live underwater and have gills are fish. Find the missing sticker, then circle all the fish you see.

Science

Learning Seasons! Find the missing sticker, then circle the things that belong in summer.

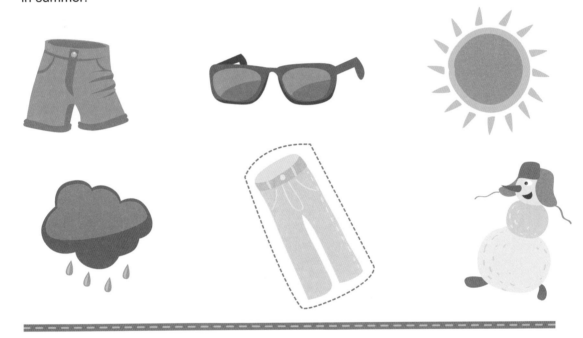

Learning Seasons! Find the missing sticker, then circle the things that belong in fall.

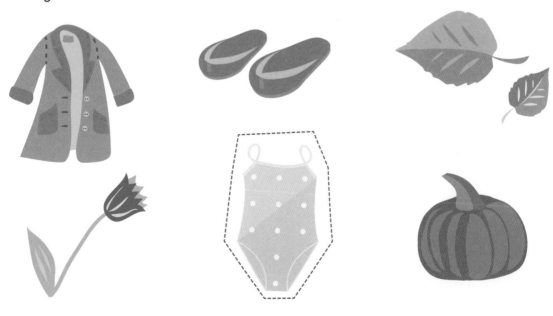

Science

Learning Seasons! Find the missing sticker, then circle the things that belong in winter.

Learning Seasons! Find the missing sticker, then circle the things that belong in spring.

Memory Game and Flashcards

Animal Alphabet Memory Game

Cut out the cards along the dotted line and shuffle. Then, place them facedown on the floor or table. If you're playing with one or more friends, take turns. On your turn, flip two cards over. If the cards don't match, place them facedown in the same spot. Now it's the next player's turn. If the letters match, remove the cards and continue until you don't find a pair. Whoever finds the most pairs wins!

Numbers Flashcards

Cut out the flashcards along the dotted line. Practice counting the animals on each card. Flip the cards over to check your answers. Quiz yourself or play with a friend!

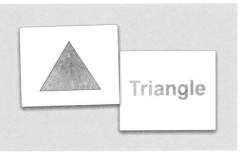

Shapes Flashcards

Cut out the flashcards along the dotted line. Practice recognizing and naming shapes. Flip the card over at any time to see if you're right!

Colors Flashcards

Cut out the flashcards along the dotted line. Practice recognizing and naming colors. Flip the card over at any time to see if you're right!

Animal Alphabet Memory Game

Alligator   alligator   **B**ear   **b**ear

Camel   Camel   **D**olphin   **d**olphin

Elephant   elephant   Frog   frog

Animal Alphabet Memory Game

Animal Alphabet

Memory Game

Animal Alphabet

Memory Game

Animal Alphabet

Memory Game

Animal Alphabet

Memory Game

Animal Alphabet

Memory Game

Animal Alphabet

Memory Game

Animal Alphabet

Memory Game

Animal Alphabet

Memory Game

Animal Alphabet

Memory Game

Animal Alphabet

Memory Game

Animal Alphabet

Memory Game

Animal Alphabet

Memory Game

Animal Alphabet Memory Game

Giraffe	giraffe	Hippo	hippo
Iguana	iguana	Jaguar	jaguar
Koala	Koala	Lion	lion

Animal Alphabet Memory Game

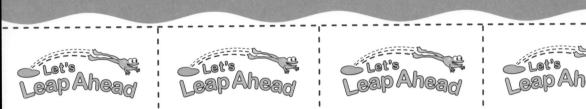

Let's Leap Ahead	Let's Leap Ahead	Let's Leap Ahead	Let's Leap Ahead
Animal Alphabet	**Animal Alphabet**	**Animal Alphabet**	**Animal Alphabet**
Memory Game	Memory Game	Memory Game	Memory Game
Let's Leap Ahead	Let's Leap Ahead	Let's Leap Ahead	Let's Leap Ahead
Animal Alphabet	**Animal Alphabet**	**Animal Alphabet**	**Animal Alphabet**
Memory Game	Memory Game	Memory Game	Memory Game
Let's Leap Ahead	Let's Leap Ahead	Let's Leap Ahead	Let's Leap Ahead
Animal Alphabet	**Animal Alphabet**	**Animal Alphabet**	**Animal Alphabet**
Memory Game	Memory Game	Memory Game	Memory Game

Animal Alphabet Memory Game

Monkey	monkey	**N**ewt	newt
Octopus	octopus	**P**enguin	penguin
Quail	quail	**R**hino	rhino

Animal Alphabet Memory Game

Let's Leap Ahead

Animal Alphabet

Memory Game

Animal Alphabet

Memory Game

Animal Alphabet

Memory Game

Animal Alphabet

Memory Game

Let's Leap Ahead

Animal Alphabet

Memory Game

Animal Alphabet

Memory Game

Animal Alphabet

Memory Game

Animal Alphabet

Memory Game

Let's Leap Ahead

Animal Alphabet

Memory Game

Animal Alphabet

Memory Game

Animal Alphabet

Memory Game

Animal Alphabet

Memory Game

Animal Alphabet Memory Game

Snake	Snake	Tiger	tiger

Urial	Urial	Vulture	Vulture

Walrus	Walrus	Xenops	Xenops

Animal Alphabet Memory Game

Let's Leap Ahead

Animal Alphabet

Memory Game

Let's Leap Ahead

Animal Alphabet

Memory Game

Let's Leap Ahead

Animal Alphabet

Memory Game

Let's Leap Ahead

Animal Alphabet

Memory Game

Let's Leap Ahead

Animal Alphabet

Memory Game

Let's Leap Ahead

Animal Alphabet

Memory Game

Let's Leap Ahead

Animal Alphabet

Memory Game

Let's Leap Ahead

Animal Alphabet

Memory Game

Let's Leap Ahead

Animal Alphabet

Memory Game

Let's Leap Ahead

Animal Alphabet

Memory Game

Let's Leap Ahead

Animal Alphabet

Memory Game

Let's Leap Ahead

Animal Alphabet

Memory Game

Animal Alphabet Memory Game

Yak   **y**ak   **Z**ebra   **Z**ebra

Animal Alphabet Memory Game

Animal Alphabet

Memory Game

Animal Alphabet

Memory Game

Animal Alphabet

Memory Game

Animal Alphabet

Memory Game

Numbers Flashcards

Numbers Flashcards

1	One
2	Two
3	Three

Numbers Flashcards

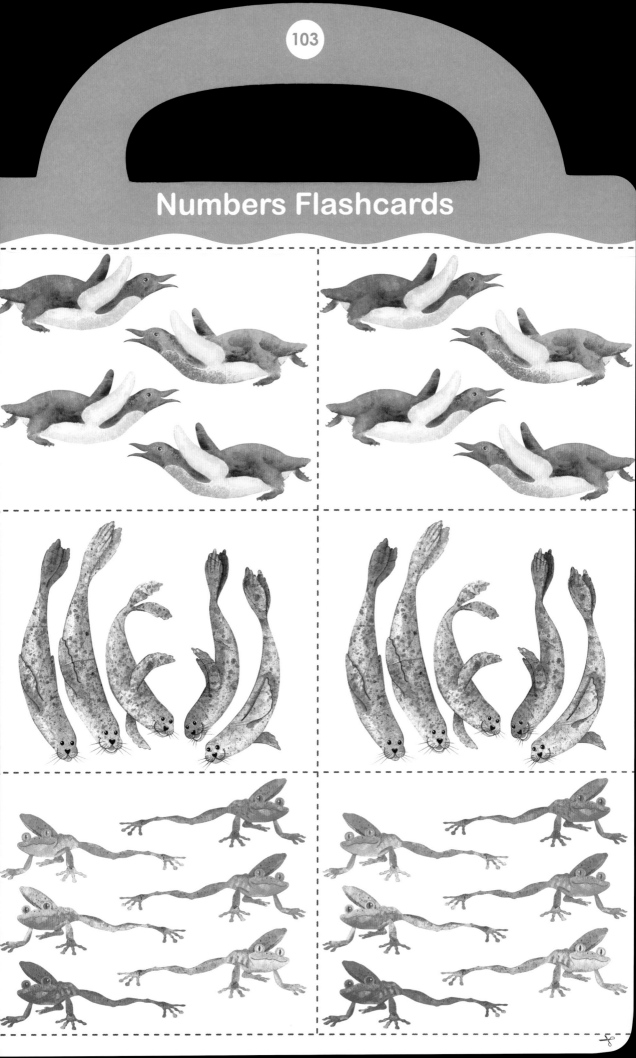

Numbers Flashcards

4

Four

5

Five

6

Six

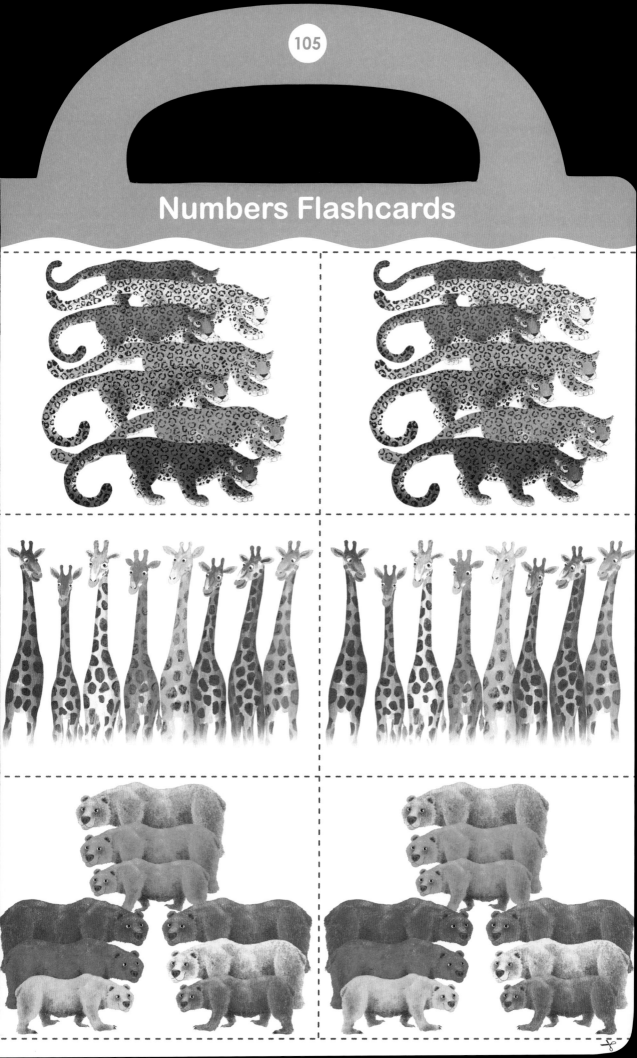

Numbers Flashcards

Numbers Flashcards

 Seven

 Eight

 Nine

Numbers Flashcards

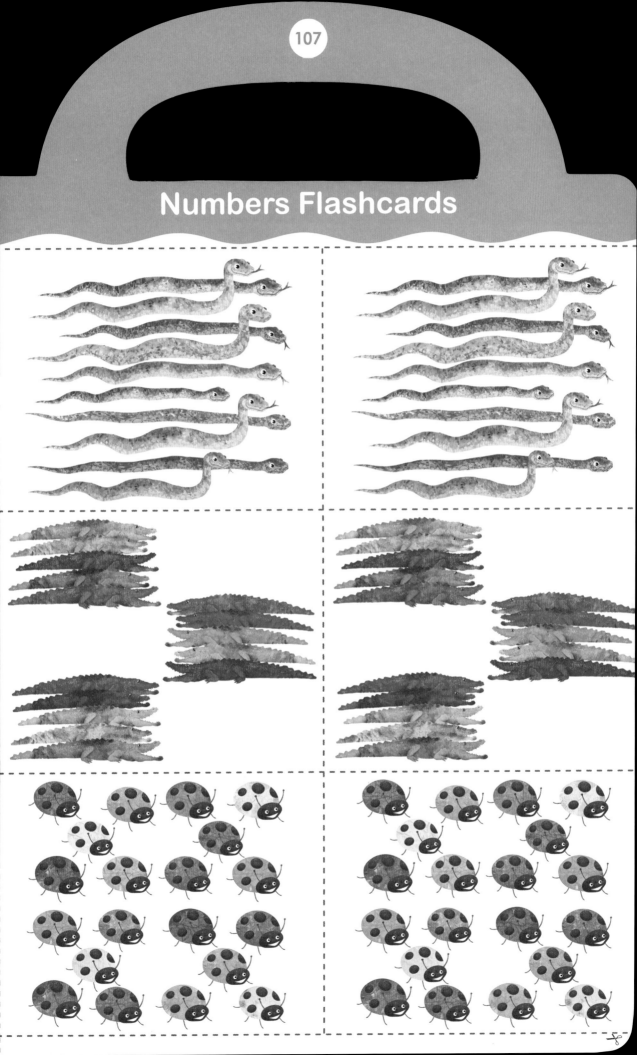

Numbers Flashcards

10	Ten
15	Fifteen
20	Twenty

Shapes Flashcards

Shapes Flashcards

Diamond	**Circle**
Square	**Oval**
Rectangle	**Triangle**

Shapes Flashcards

Shapes Flashcards

Star	Trapezoid
Pentagon	Heart
Octagon	Hexagon

Colors Flashcards

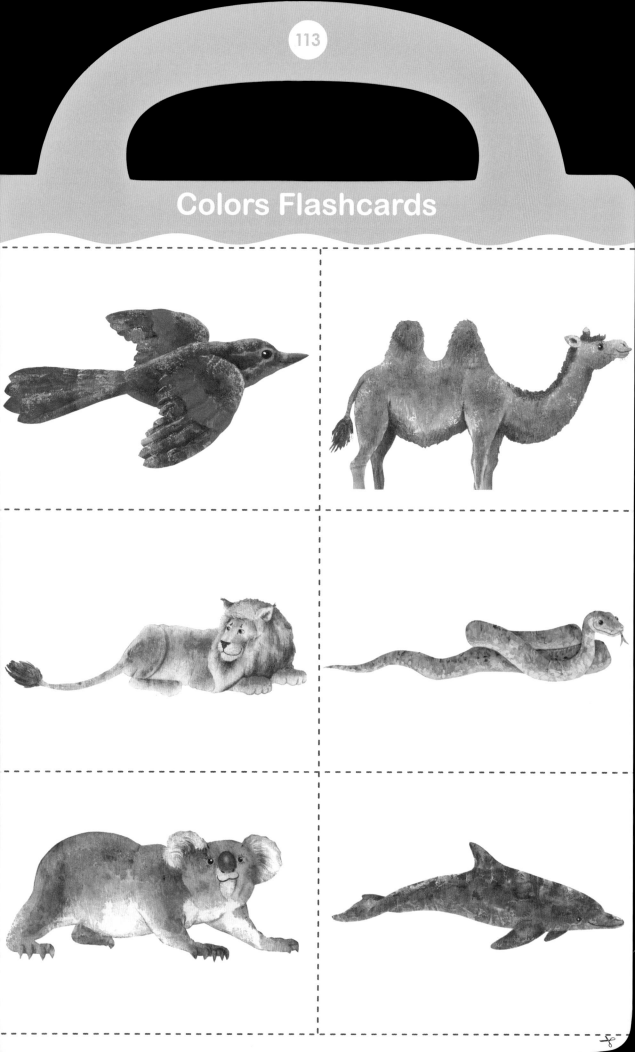

Colors Flashcards

Orange	Red
Green	Yellow
Purple	Blue

Colors Flashcards

Colors Flashcards

Pink	**Teal**
Brown	**Lime**
White	**Black**